Published by DC Thomson Annuals Ltd in 2013

DC Thomson Annuals Ltd., 185 Fleet Street, London EC4A 2HS

© DC Thomson & Co. Ltd. 2013

For great comic gift ideas, visit www.dcthomson.co.uk
and click on Gift Ideas. Or call 0800 318846
(overseas +44 1382 575580). Lines open 8am – 9pm, 7 days.

Loaded with laughs, packed with stories and filled with extras,
videos and games – it's the next-generation comic you won't
want to miss!

www.dandy.com

BANANAMAN!

There's a nasty niff in town today – I wonder what's happening?

It's getting worse – I don't know how people can stand it!

Crumbs! It looks like they can't!"

My dog's got no nose – so he's okay!

This is a job for Bananaman!

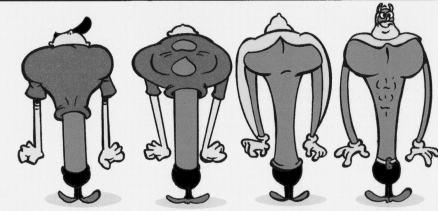

Whew! I think I'm getting closer to the scene of the crime!

So, it's Sammy the Sprout – the Foul-smellin' Felon! Up to your old tricks again, Sammy?

Bananaman! Who scent you to stop me?

I'm my own boss, Sammy. Now brace yourself – this town is about to be de-ponged!

KORKY the CAT

Nigel Auchterlounie

Poor Figaro has been stuck in thees jail for many years.

Oh, when will he get out?

Still here, Figaro? This door's been unlocked for two years - we thought you'd gone.

Many curses!

And remember not to commit any more crimes!

Right after I rob ze train!

Figaro is hurt you think he go back to criminal ways! He is on ze straight an' ze narrow from now on!

Even with Figaro's highly intelligent brains, zis timetable is mucho complicated!

I think ze train carrying ze moneys is coming zis afternoon.

Zis should be as easy as stealing ze tortilla from ze baby!

Hup! Such grace Figaro possesses!

Zis is going exactly as planned.

Now to get inside ze train, steal ze moneys and leap back onto my horse once more. So simple!

Ze tunnel! But Figaro will not be stopped! Thees feels like ze bag of moneys.

QUALITY HORSE MANURE

HUP!

Money has changed a leetle bit while I was in ze jail.

And it no smell so good.

Alexander Matthews

MY DAD'S A DOOFUS!

Right, you've all been in my cookery class for years, and you're all still TERRIBLE at cooking!

So, you have ONE HOUR to create a delicious signature dish. Prove to me we haven't all been wasting our time!

One hour later...

I made a TURNIP!

I'm wearing my pudding.

I think mine's on the ceiling.

I baked my hand into my cake.

It hurts.

Be ready in a minute!

Ty's Dad, what on earth are you cooking?

Oh, you'll see.

You'll all see.

MIX! MIX!

My world-famous, secret recipe signature dish...

BLACK PUDDING!

EWW!!

Oh, don't be soft. This'll put hairs on your chest! I added extra grit, pig trotters and flotsam, for texture!

GRRRR!

That's funny, it never growled before.

You pass! You all pass cookery class! Just call it off!

There there! Down, boy!

GRRNCKK!!

JAM16

NICK KELLY
Special Agent
And his assistant
CEDRIC
In the Disappearance of Agent Muffins!

Ah, agent Kelly and Cedric. Come in. It's bad news, I'm afraid.

What's the problem, Minister?

Agent Muffins has gone missing.

Oh no! When was he last seen?

This morning. I found him asleep on that filing cabinet behind me.

He then chased a fly for ten minutes before scratching the door frame a bit.

No one's seen him since.

Er...

Is Agent Muffins your cat, sir?

Oh! A cat! Ha ha! That explains it! I thought...

Er... It doesn't matter what I thought. We're on the case, Minister, don't you worry.

I have a secret meeting with the Prime Minister, Kelly. Find that cat!

You can rely on us, Minister, we'll have Agent Muffins back to you before you know it!

First thing we need to do, Cedric, is get this computer on.

Why?

CLICKY CLICK

To look for another job. How on Earth am I meant to find a cat!?!

You're not even going to try?

Hrrrgh! Right! Ok! We'll give it a go.

Nigel Auchterlounie

...Followed with less confidence by Cedric.

Yikes!

He's gone round the corner!

Meanwhile, close by...

Posing as the cleaners of windows is excellent way for enemy agents such as ourselves to listen in on secret meetings.

Yes, comrade. Very much so.

What can you hear, brother?

It is typical British Secret Service meeting.

Many are complaining about the biscuits that have been bought for the meeting.

One of them is saying that when he worked for the Department for Transport they used to have custard creams for meetings...

Someone else is saying that bourbons are better.

Such decadence!

Now it is being said that wagon wheels used to be bigger.

Now man who thinks he is cat is walking past!

Meow!

?

My years as Kraznovian secret agent have taught me how strange these English are!

Is true, comrade!

Those enemy agents think us Brits are all weirdos, eh? I can use that to my advantage!

Good day to you, gentlemen! A fine day for a stroll along a high ledge, don't you think?

JIBBER AND Steve

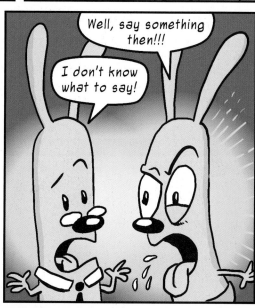

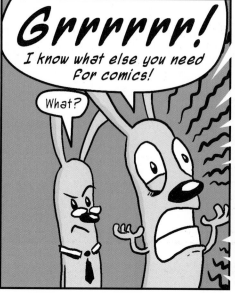

Nigel Auchterlounie

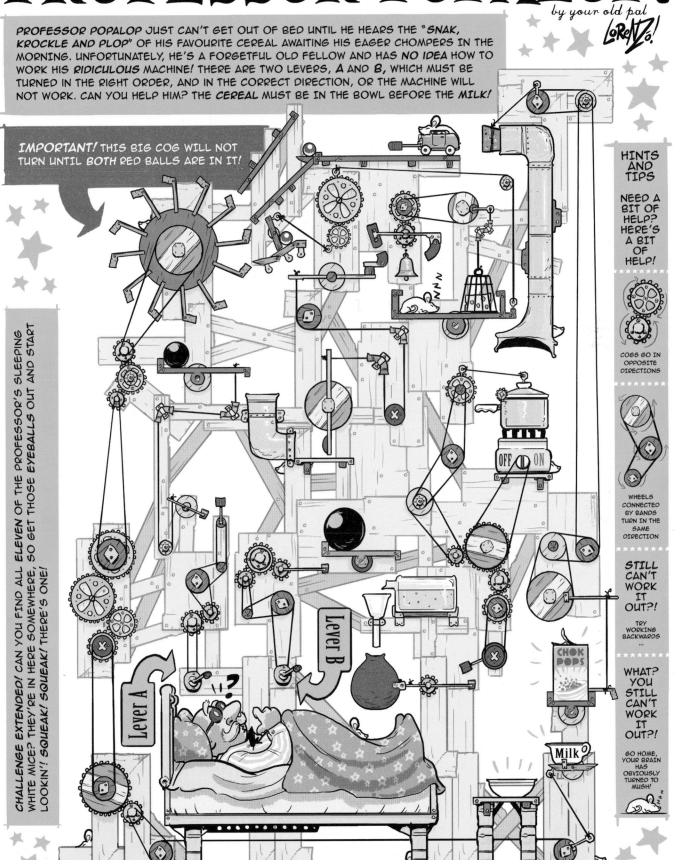

PROFESSOR POPALOP!

by your old pal **Lorenzo!**

PROFESSOR POPALOP JUST CAN'T GET OUT OF BED UNTIL HE HEARS THE "SNAK, KROCKLE AND PLOP" OF HIS FAVOURITE CEREAL AWAITING HIS EAGER CHOMPERS IN THE MORNING. UNFORTUNATELY, HE'S A FORGETFUL OLD FELLOW AND HAS *NO IDEA* HOW TO WORK HIS *RIDICULOUS* MACHINE! THERE ARE TWO LEVERS, A AND B, WHICH MUST BE TURNED IN THE RIGHT ORDER, AND IN THE CORRECT DIRECTION, OR THE MACHINE WILL NOT WORK. CAN YOU HELP HIM? THE *CEREAL* MUST BE IN THE BOWL BEFORE THE *MILK!*

IMPORTANT! THIS BIG COG WILL NOT TURN UNTIL *BOTH* RED BALLS ARE IN IT!

CHALLENGE EXTENDED! CAN YOU FIND ALL *ELEVEN* OF THE PROFESSOR'S SLEEPING WHITE MICE? THEY'RE IN HERE SOMEWHERE, SO GET THOSE EYEBALLS OUT AND START LOOKIN'! SQUEAK! SQUEAK! THERE'S ONE!

Lever A

Lever B

OFF ON

CHOK POPS

Milk

HINTS AND TIPS

NEED A BIT OF HELP? HERE'S A BIT OF HELP!

COGS GO IN OPPOSITE DIRECTIONS

WHEELS CONNECTED BY BANDS TURN IN THE SAME DIRECTION

STILL CAN'T WORK IT OUT?!

TRY WORKING BACKWARDS ...

WHAT? YOU STILL CAN'T WORK IT OUT?!

GO HOME, YOUR BRAIN HAS OBVIOUSLY TURNED TO MUSH!

KORKY the CAT

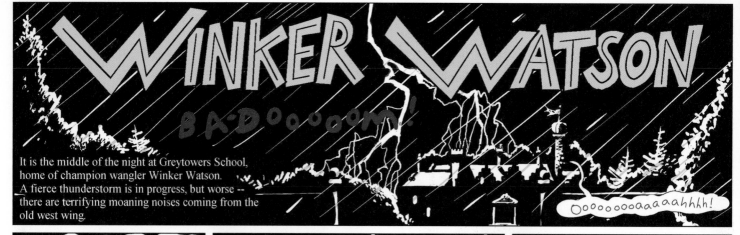

WINKER WATSON

BA-DOOOOOM!

It is the middle of the night at Greytowers School, home of champion wangler Winker Watson. A fierce thunderstorm is in progress, but worse -- there are terrifying moaning noises coming from the old west wing.

Oooooooaaaaahhh!

Oooooooaaaaahhh!

Listen to that!

I haven't been so petrified since Father was made redundant and threatened to send me to the local comprehensive!

I can't bear it!

Oh, don't worry, he got another job.

He means the moaning from the west wing, you idiot.

We'll have to wake Winker. He'll know what to do.

Cripes! I see what you mean, chaps. That's s-s-scary! I hate to admit it, but I think we're going to need an adult to deal with this. Let's go and find Creepy.

Oooooooaaaaahhh!

I've never seen Winker defeated before!

Well, it took a *supernatural* being to do it!

You don't *really* think it's a ghost, do you?

Mr C-Creep, sir! We're all terrified! There's a ghost in the w-west wing!

KA-BOOOM!

A g-g-ghost?! Don't be silly boy!

Come and listen, sir -- it's wailing to wake the dead.

Wait a minute, where's Watson?

BULLY BEEF AND CHIPS

Oh no! Bully Beef is coming!

Eek! And Porky Puncher too! I'm doomed!

I'll have to pretend to pick flowers and hope they don't see me!

Oh, dear. Picking FLOWERS, Chips?"

That means I LEGALLY have to give you a grade A thumping! It's in the rules!

They're for my mum!

BULLYING CHARTER

Your MUM?!?

Yes! Why not?

Sniff! I'll pick some for my mum too... THEN I'll punch your lights out!

Bully Beef? Picking soppy flowers?!?

You know the rules, Beefy!

Hang on! It's not what it looks like!

FLOWER 'bout I give you a VERY special thumping?

His nose is bright red, his bruises are new.

By the time Porky's finished, Beef will look black and blue!

SSBeckett

CORPORAL CLOTT

I don't think Ninjas run around actually saying "Ninja Ninja!"-Ed.

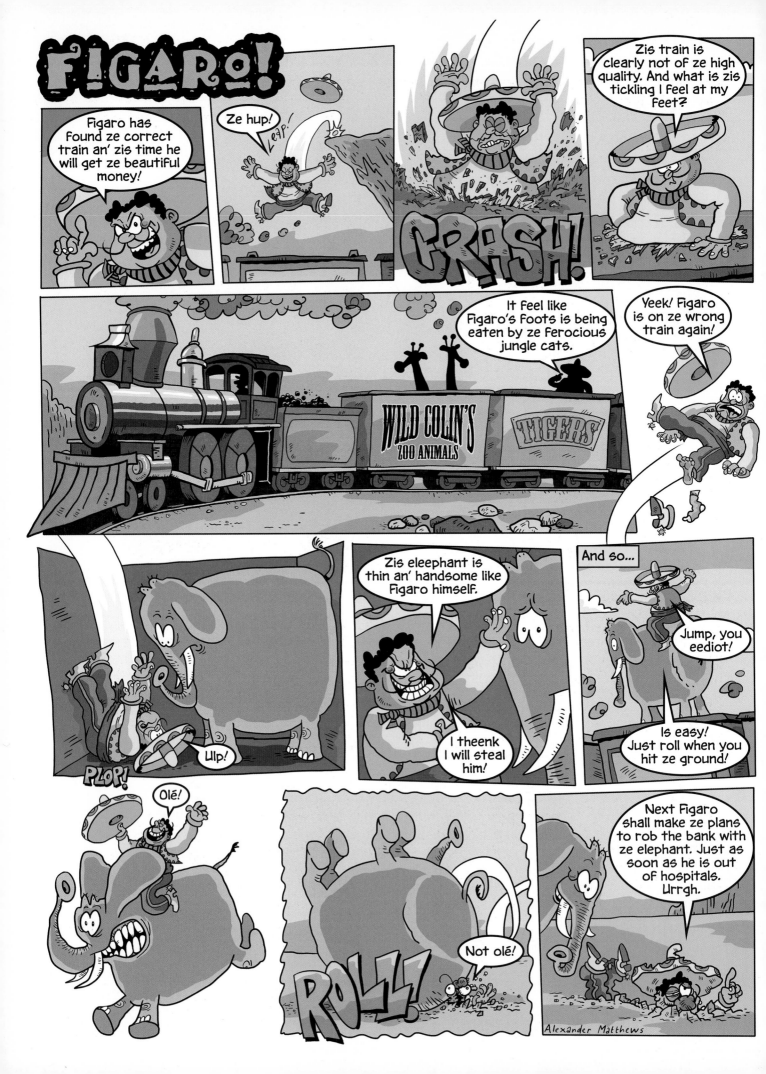

PROFESSOR POPALOP!

by your old pal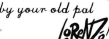

OOH! PROFESSOR POPALOP'S NEW *"PUDDLE STEPPER"* ROBOTIC WALKER IS NEARLY READY! WHOOP! BUT THE PROF'S ASSISTANT, *FANGLES*, SEEMS TO HAVE BROUGHT HIM THE WRONG PART TO FINISH THE JOB! CAN YOU TELL WHICH IS THE *CORRECT* LEG?

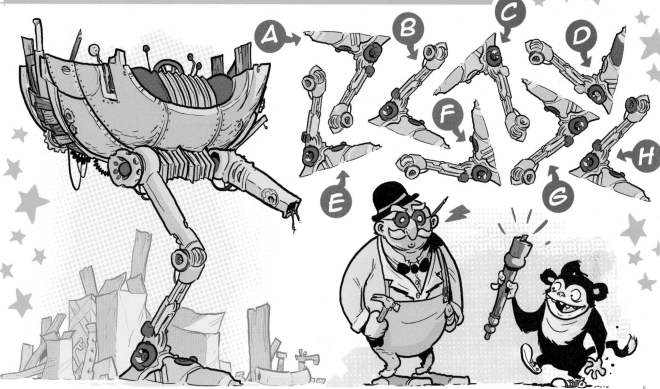

TIME TO FIX THAT LEG ON! THERE ARE THREE BARRELS: ONE CONTAINING *NUTS*, ONE CONTAINING *BOLTS*, AND ONE CONTAINING *COGS*. FANGLES PUT LABELS ON THEM BUT FANGLES IS *STUPID*, AND NOW *NONE* OF THE BARRELS HAS THE RIGHT LABEL. THE PROF SAYS HE CAN TELL WHAT ALL THE BARRELS HAVE IN THEM *JUST* BY LOOKING IN THE BARREL MARKED *NUTS*. HOW?

NUTS   BOLTS   COGS

THE PROF HAS CROSSED HIS WIRES! WHICH TWO ARE CONNECTED TO THE LEG?

SOLUTIONS: MISSING LEG: **G** IS THE CORRECT ONE.

THE BARRELS: REMEMBER, ALL THE BARRELS HAVE THE WRONG LABELS ON THEM, SO IF THE PROFESSOR LOOKS IN THE NUTS BARREL HE WILL EITHER FIND BOLTS OR COGS. IF HE FINDS BOLTS HE THEN KNOWS THAT THE BARREL MARKED COGS MUST CONTAIN NUTS, AS THE COGS BARREL CAN'T CONTAIN COGS (CALL THE LABELS ARE WRONG, REMEMBER?), THAT LEAVES THE BOLTS BARREL, WHICH MUST CONTAIN THE COGS! IF HE FINDS COGS IN THE NUTS BARREL HE CAN WORK IT OUT SIMILARLY, EXCEPT THIS TIME THE BARREL MARKED BOLTS WOULD CONTAIN NUTS AND THE BARREL MARKED COGS WOULD CONTAIN BOLTS. EASY, HUH? WHAT DO YOU MEAN YOUR BRAIN JUST MELTED?!

CROSSED WIRES: WIRES 1 AND 3 ARE THE CORRECT ONES.

NICK KELLY Special Agent

And his assistant CEDRIC In Agents of Change!

"Ah, Agent Kelly and Cedric. I have an important mission for you both."

"These two vans are full of new-fangled weapons from our experimental weapons division..."

"I need you to drive them to our high security warehouse."

"The last thing we need is enemy agents getting hold of them."

"Okay, Cedric. I'll take the lead van, you follow me. Okay?"

"Okay. Just one thing..."

"Where's the other van?"

"Stolen!!!"

SPACE!!!

"Enemy agents!"

"Quick! After them!"

SCREECH!

"Ha ha! A clean getaway! Those British fools will soon discover their flat tyres!"

"Flat tyres?"

"I was supposed to let the tyres down on the other van, wasn't I?"

"That's the trouble with identical vans. Ours isn't faster."

"I'll see what we have in the back to slow them down."

"I don't know what any of these things do!"

"Just try anything!"

"So Cedric tries something..."

ZAP!

Cedric tries a different weapon.

The tiny enemy agents try something else first.

Nigel Auchterlounie

MY DAD'S A DOOFUS!

I'm really worried about the big test today, Dad. Have you studied for it?

Pah! Don't need to.

I stayed behind last night, and wrote KEY FACTS on strategic parts of the classroom walls!

1492 - AMERICA DISCOVERED

WATER = H_2O

BANANA IS A HERB

With this knowledge, I can answer any question and ACE THE TEST!

Right! Test begins NOW!

I'm not sure this is a good idea, Dad.

PFFT!

Number 26... Ah! The answer to that is on the ceiling, left corner.

Number 42... oh yes, back wall, halfway down...

I am a GENIUS!

Next day...

Everyone did well in the test EXCEPT for Ty's Dad.

What? It can't be! I had ALL the answers...

...written down.

Number 13 answer: "Twittown F.C. ROOLZ!"

Number 29 answer: "Let's 'ave a fight!"

Number 32 answer: "Ty wears a frilly dress!"

Hoi!

Sorry.

But I don't understand! I was reading everything straight off the wall.

...including...

...the BONEHEAD TWINS' GRAFFITI!

$4 \times 4 = 16$

1523

YOU IS UGLY!

MARIE ANTOINE

BIG BUMS

Sighhh.

GRRR!

Hur hur.

what?

JAMIE

The SMASHER

ANTIQUES FAYRE TODAY!!
FREE ADMISSION

LOADS OF DUSTY OLD RELICS
→ AND THAT'S JUST THE DEALERS.

Oho! This could be fun!

OH NO! IT'S THE SMASHER!

AAGH! Things always get smashed when he's around!

You won't get my grandfather clock! No way!

Gasp! This is heavy! OOPS! Sorry!

My Victorian china!

BUMP!

SMASH!

Oi! You owe me!

Wahh! Don't push!

SMASH!

My Roman coins!

You're not getting near my rare crystal swordfish! No way, no how!

?

Guess where those coins have landed!

WAHHH!

SLIP!

...and here we have an early Van Gobrant painting which is worth...

RRIPP!

...nothing now!

EXIT

Some days I don't even need to try!

LEW STRINGER

CUDDLES and DIMPLES

BANANAMAN!

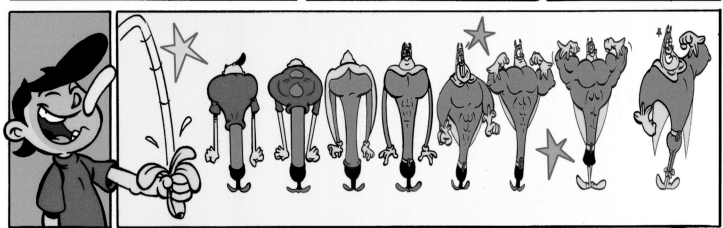

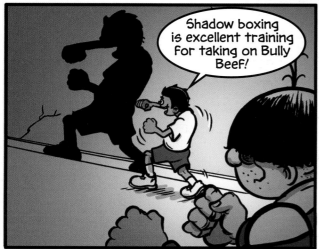

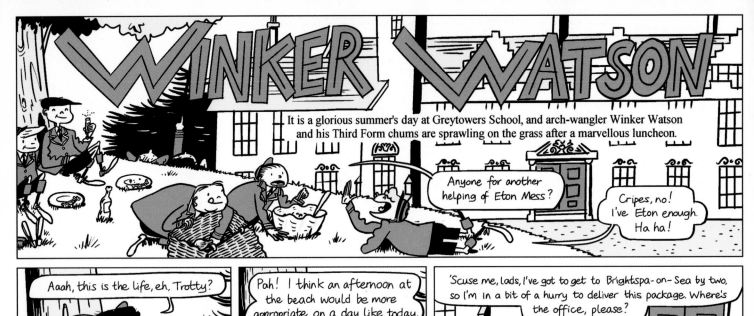

WINKER WATSON

It is a glorious summer's day at Greytowers School, and arch-wangler Winker Watson and his Third Form chums are sprawling on the grass after a marvellous luncheon.

Anyone for another helping of Eton Mess?

Cripes, no! I've Eton enough. Ha ha!

Aaah, this is the life, eh, Trotty?

It certainly is, Winker. Just a shame we've got double Biology this afternoon.

Pah! I think an afternoon at the beach would be more appropriate on a day like today, don't you, old bean?

'Scuse me, lads, I've got to get to Brightspa-on-Sea by two, so I'm in a bit of a hurry to deliver this package. Where's the office, please?

R. SMYTHE
COURIER

Spot of luck!

We'll have a smashing time at the beach, chaps, and be back in time for supper!

But Winker--

Don't worry, Boffo. Winker will fix it so no-one gets in trouble.

Oh I know that, Trotty. It's just that the forecast was for rain this afternoon.

R. SMYTHE
COURIER

We're here, men. Quickly, now.

Sorry I don't have anything larger.

I'll join you in a jiffy, chaps. Squiffy, does your uncle still run the Brightspa Natural History Museum?

TELEPHONE

KORKY the CAT

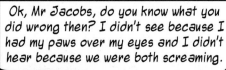

PROFESSOR POPALOP!

by your old pal
LoReNZo!

PROFESSOR POPALOP HAS DECIDED THAT HIS ASSISTANT, *FANGLES*, COULD DO WITH BEING A BIT BIGGER, FOR REACHING STUFF ON HIGH SHELVES AND THINGS LIKE THAT. THE PROBLEM IS, HE'S NOT SURE IF HE'S MIXED THE *RIGHT* FORMULA TO MAKE FANGLES GROW! YIKES! BY LOOKING AT ALL THE *BOTTLES* HE HAS LEFT OVER, AND THE *RECIPES* FOR HIS VARIOUS FORMULAS, CAN YOU TELL WHAT THE PROFESSOR HAS MADE?

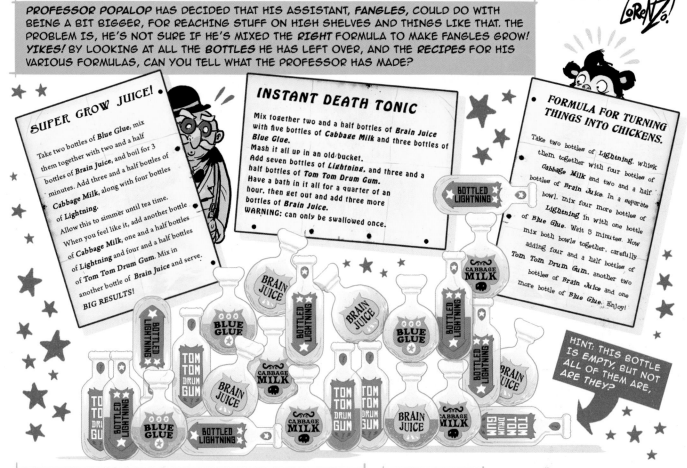

SUPER GROW JUICE!

Take two bottles of *Blue Glue*, mix them together with two and a half bottles of *Brain Juice*, and boil for 3 minutes. Add three and a half bottles of *Cabbage Milk*, along with four bottles of *Lightning*.

Allow this to simmer until tea time. When you feel like it, add another bottle of *Cabbage Milk*, one and a half bottles of *Lightning* and four and a half bottles of *Tom Tom Drum Gum*. Mix in another bottle of *Brain Juice* and serve.

BIG RESULTS!

INSTANT DEATH TONIC

Mix together two and a half bottles of *Brain Juice* with five bottles of *Cabbage Milk* and three bottles of *Blue Glue*.

Mash it all up in an old bucket. Add seven bottles of *Lightning*, and three and a half bottles of *Tom Tom Drum Gum*. Have a bath in it all for a quarter of an hour, then get out and add three more bottles of *Brain Juice*.

WARNING: can only be swallowed once.

FORMULA FOR TURNING THINGS INTO CHICKENS.

Take two bottles of *Lightning*, whisk them together with four bottles of *Cabbage Milk* and two and a half bottles of *Brain Juice*. In a separate bowl, mix four more bottles of *Lightning* in with one bottle of *Blue Glue*. Wait 5 minutes. Now mix both bowls together, carefully adding four and a half bottles of *Tom Tom Drum Gum*, another two bottles of *Brain Juice* and one more bottle of *Blue Glue*. Enjoy!

HINT: THIS BOTTLE IS EMPTY, BUT NOT ALL OF THEM ARE, ARE THEY?

FANGLES HAS A BAD FEELING ABOUT HIS "MEDICINE" AND DECIDES TO LEG IT! HE COMES TO A DOOR WITH *TWO* LEVERS – WHICH ONE WILL OPEN THE DOOR AND ALLOW HIM TO *ESCAPE*, AND WHICH WILL *TRAP* HIM IN A GHASTLY CAGE?

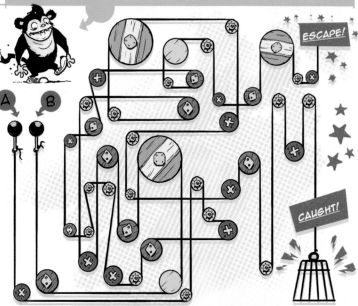

ESCAPE!

CAUGHT!

A   B

YIPES! SILLY OLD FANGLES HAS PULLED THE *WRONG* LEVER AND NOW HE'S *TRAPPED!* ARGH! THE *HORROR!* CAN YOU MOVE *THREE BARS* TO REFORM THE CAGE IN THE *SAME SHAPE*, BUT WITH FANGLES *OUTSIDE* IT?

CHALLENGE EXTENDED!

SEE IF YOU CAN DO IT BY MOVING JUST *TWO BARS!*

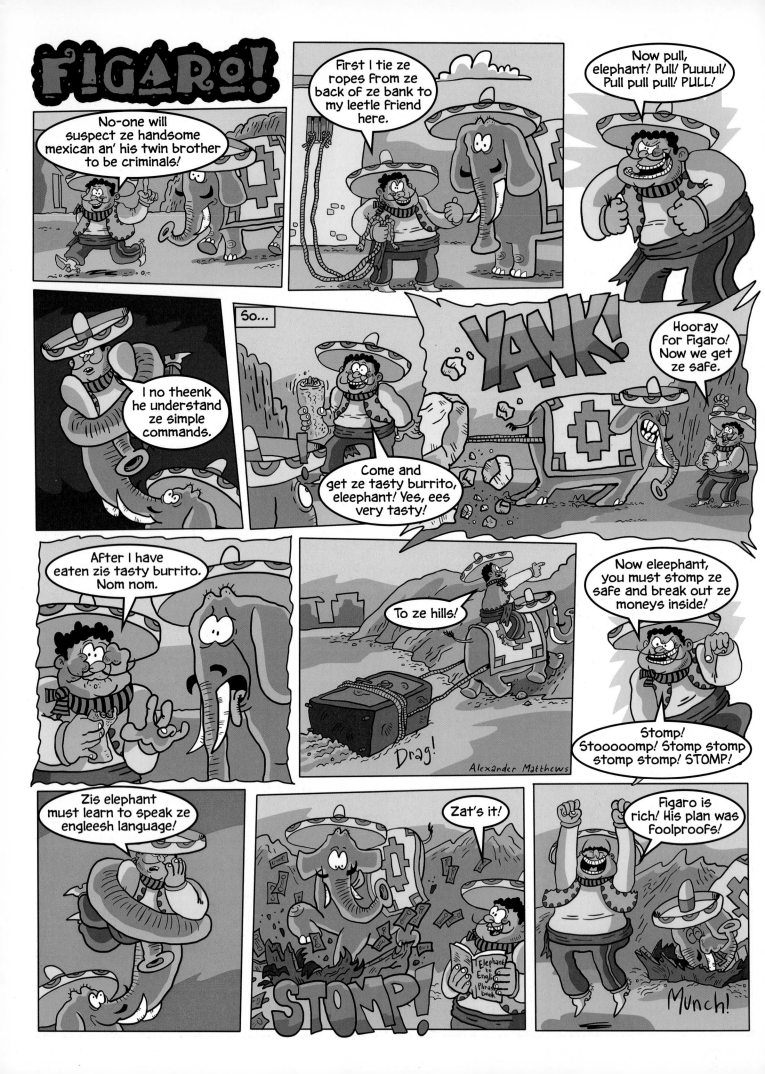

JIBBER AND Steve

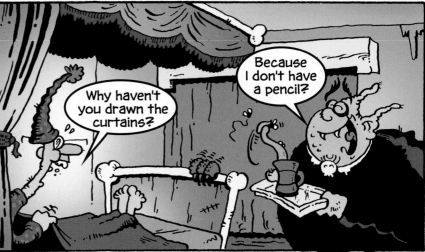

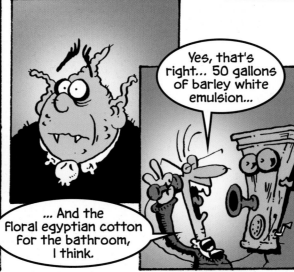

PROFESSOR POPALOP!

HOT POTATOES! PROFESSOR POPALOP HAS BUILT A **MASSIVE** AWESOME ROBOT! YEAH! THE GIANT METAL MAN IS POWERED BY SPECIAL LITTLE CREATURES CALLED **"FUFFLES"**, WHICH THE PROFESSOR ACCIDENTALLY INVENTED ONE DAY WHILST MAKING A CUP OF TEA. THE PROBLEM IS, THERE ARE **FIVE** DIFFERENT TYPES OF FUFFLE, AND THEY MUST BE INSERTED **CORRECTLY** INTO THE ROBOT'S FOURTEEN POWER SOCKETS. USING THE GUIDES FOR EACH FUFFLE, CAN YOU FIGURE OUT WHICH COLOURS GO IN WHICH SOCKETS?

IMPORTANT!

FUFFLES **CANNOT GO** IN SOCKETS WHICH ARE CONNECTED TO WIRES THE **SAME** COLOUR AS THEY ARE!

GREEN FUFFLES

- CAN ONLY GO IN SOCKETS WITH ODD NUMBERS ON THEM.

RED FUFFLES

- CAN'T GO IN SOCKETS WITH THREE WIRES CONNECTED TO THEM.
- CAN ONLY GO IN SOCKETS WITH EVEN NUMBERS ON THEM.

BLUE FUFFLES

- CAN ONLY GO IN SOCKETS WITH AT LEAST THREE WIRES CONNECTED TO THEM.
- CANNOT GO IN SOCKETS WITH EVEN NUMBERS ON THEM.

YELLOW FUFFLES

- CAN ONLY GO IN SOCKETS WITH AT LEAST ONE RED WIRE CONNECTED TO THEM.
- CANNOT GO IN SOCKETS WITH ODD NUMBERS ON THEM.
- CAN ONLY GO IN SOCKETS WITH TWO WIRES.

THE SPECIAL MAGIC **PURPLE** FUFFLE FITS INTO THE ONE SOCKET THAT NONE OF THE OTHERS CAN USE!

by your old pal LORENZO!

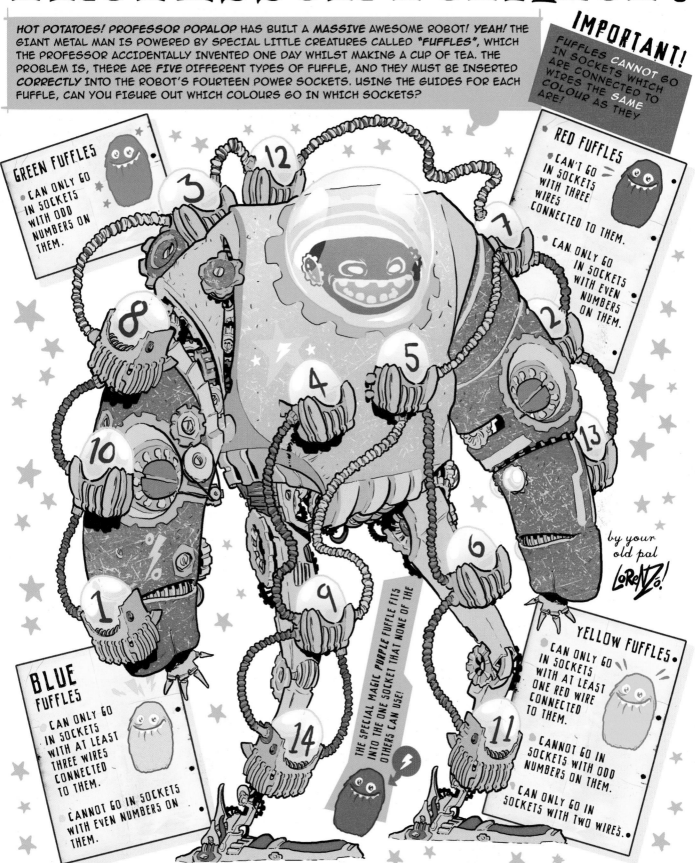

MY DAD'S A DOOFUS!

Y'know son, since this is a free period, you could be using it to do something constructive.

We are, Dad.

This is rehearsal time for our BAND!!

I'm wrapping elastic bands around each other to form a giant BALL!

why, what are YOU doing?

RIIIIGHT.

Are you SURE that's constructive?

Absolutely! When it's big enough, I'm going to run everywhere on top of it!

In fact, I wonder if I could try it now!

Dad? Dad, this is a bad idea.

Yes! YES! See you around, son! I'm off to live a life!

Your dad's weird.

SMASH!

WOOOOO

Tell me about it!

A few nights later...

SCHOOL TALENT ☆ SHOW ☆

Thank you! For our last song, we'd like to...

Sounding great, son! All that practice paying off!

Sorry!

Sorry!

Sorry!

Your dad's weird.

BYOI-NG!

ARGH!

Carry on!

Tell me about it!

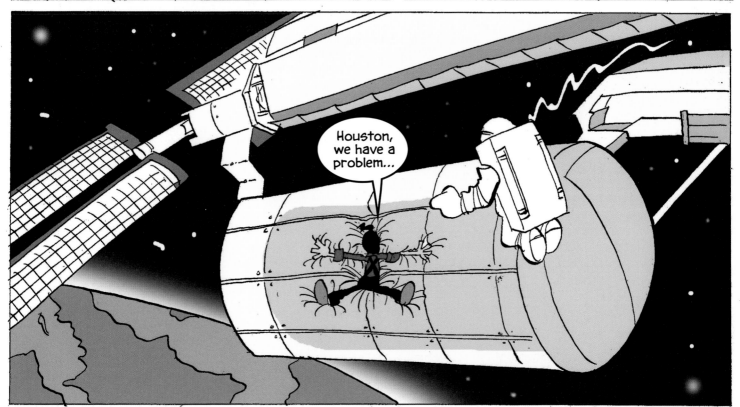

BULLY BEEF AND CHIPS

Grrr. I'm sure Chips came in here a minute ago.

Uh oh! There's Bully Beef! Better warn all my friends about this on Twitter!

TAP! TAP! TAP!

Chips doesn't know I follow him on Twitter!

BEEP! BEEP!

So he's hiding in the bird enclosure, is he?! There's no sign of him in here either.

"AM HIDING UP THE BIG TREE UNTIL BULLY BEEF HAS GONE!"

I've got him now!

Here I come, ready for a biffing or not!

What?!? Vultures?!?

Well. Well. Well. What have we here?

A nice bit of lunch, maybe?

Ha! I knew Bully Beef was following me on Twitter so I sent him false tweets!

Help! Mummy! Stop pecking me!

GROAN! Not more bloomin' tweets! I've had enough of them!

Ha! Ha! I made a twit of Bully Beef!

Curly Perkins had always wanted to travel, but had only ever been as far as Wigan. So he was pretty excited to be whisked off to outer space, to a planet called Marsuvia, home of his cool pal...

JACK SILVER

They don't half sell some weird stuff in that shop, Jack.

Weird and wonderful, Curly, mate! And just the things we'll need on our trip to the Outer Regions to see the migration of the rare Lesser-Spotted Floogly Flaaatstippler bird.

Look at those mountains, Curly. That's where we're headed. Nothing like a few days of fresh air and open countryside, eh?

Er, we have got plenty of biscuits, right, Jack?

Ah, this is the life, eh, Curly?

I can't find the biscuits...

If you're hungry, have some Marsuvian powdered food. Just a couple of grains, no more. A little goes a long way.

Just add water...

Wow!

Bleah!

Zah! I knew I should've got Barbecued Groobard flavour.

Alright, then, I'll show you something else.

I'm sure they grow around here...

Biscuits?

Aha! Here we are! The drumstickle plant! You're going to love these.

Lots of drumstickle fruits and not many biscuits later...

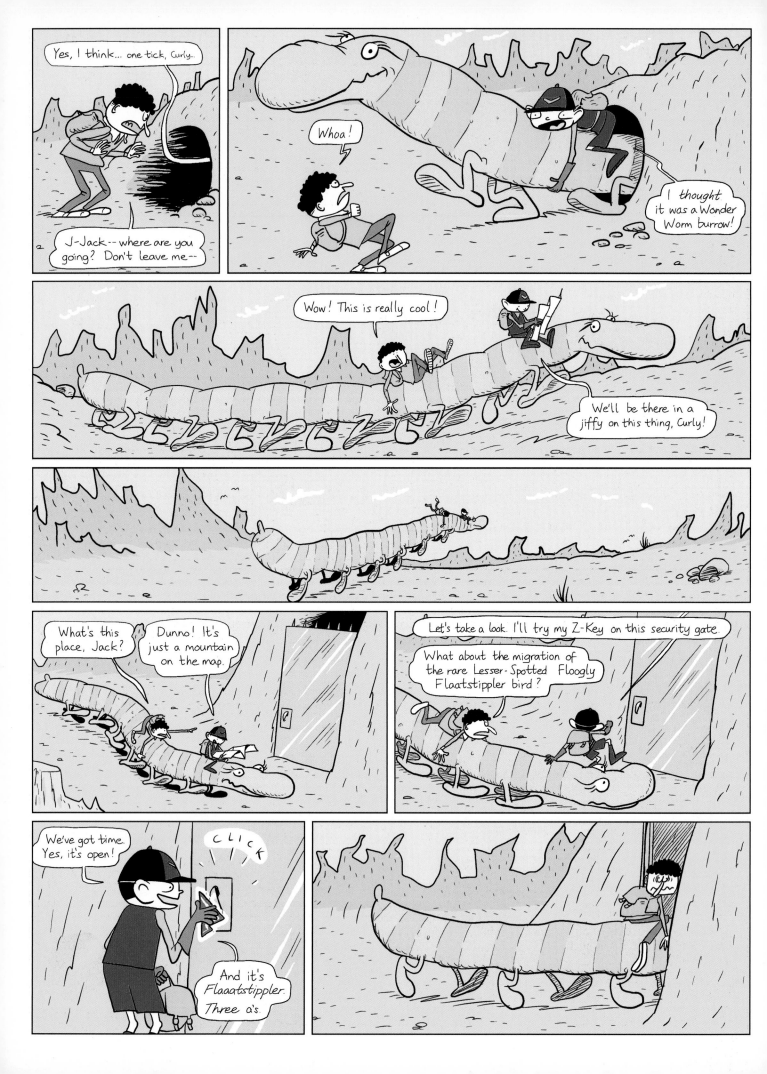

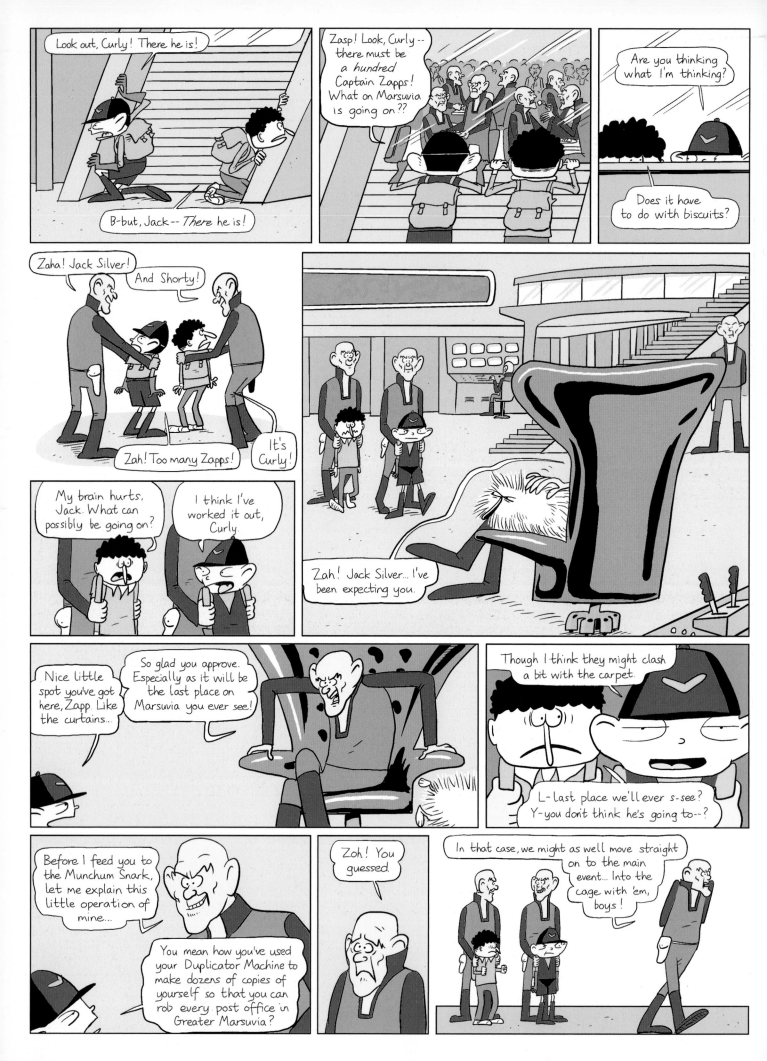

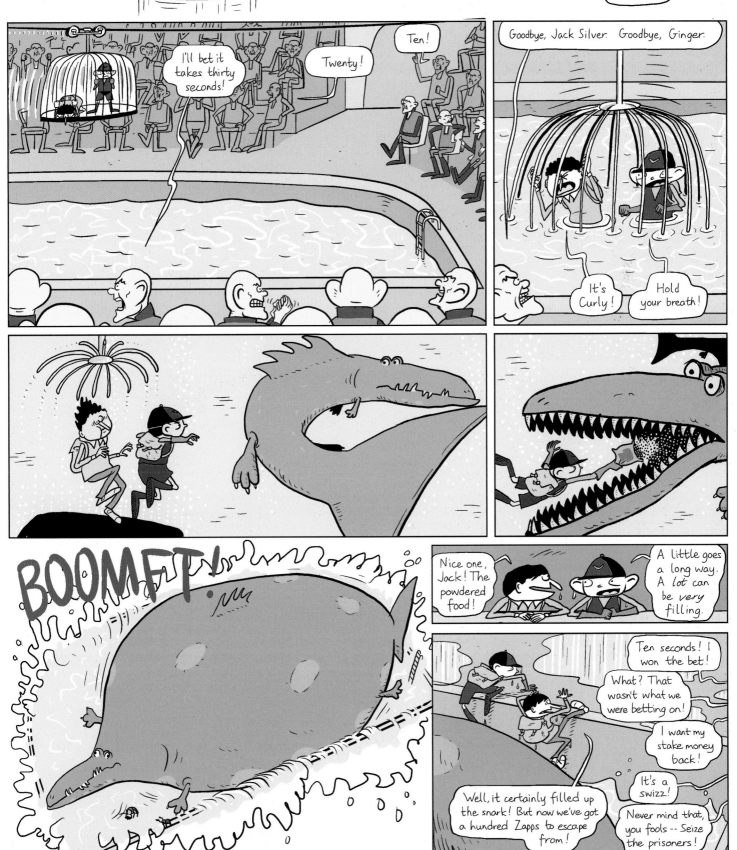

VISIT MARSUVIA

WITH SUVITOURS

14-DAY TOUR

Come to Marsuvia for the holiday of a lifetime!
Our 14-night package tour will give you and your family an amazing, unforgettable experience.

7-DAY SIGHT-SEEING TOUR

Explore the wonders of Marsuvia on this 7-day sight-seeing tour.
Including...

The floating city of Hoverchi. Hoverchi kids don't have to go to school. School comes to them!

The Skyfull Tower. A tower so tall, at the top the air is too thin to breathe. (Rest assured there is a handy shop selling Fresh Air at very reasonable prices.*)

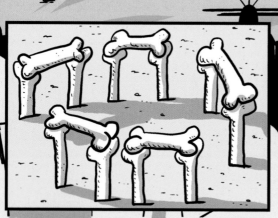

Bonehenge. An ancient monument, thought to have been made from the bones of a now extinct species of gigantic reptile. (Please note, dogs are not allowed to visit the monument)

Sunbathe on the fabulous beach at Marsukesh. When one of Marsuvia's suns goes down, don't worry, the other one will stay up a while longer!

*Please note, when we say very reasonable, we mean, of course, *not* very reasonable at all.

7-DAY SAFARI CRUISE

Then, board one of our magnificent luxury Hover Cruisers for the second leg of this Marsuper trip!

Marsuvian wildlife is famed throughout space! Some of the fabulous creatures you will be observing include:

The Yellaphunt. This large land animal has a call so loud the sound can travel all the way around the planet and surprise the very creature which made it.

The Zub-Zub Garfoonkelzopper. This peculiar bird is best known for the unusual flight formation assumed by family groups.

The Urban Googlus. This strange creature has evolved to live entirely on waste from the technological industries, and has a diet mainly of microchips. As a result, it has been useful to many a homework-laden schoolchild.

The Sabre-Toothed Shnirklebuster. This aggressive-looking creature is far less fearsome than it looks. It is a gentle vegetarian whose dagger-sharp fangs have evolved only to peel fruit and get those annoying pips out of the fleepal fruit.

THE HOLIDAY OF A LIFETIME*

*Please note, depending on where you are travelling from, and the carrier you are using, it may *take a lifetime* to *reach* Marsuvia. Space is a big place, y'know.

BING BANG BENNY

FIGARO!

KORKY the CAT

WINKER WATSON

The world's wiliest wangler prepares himself for a new day at Greytowers School. But he is *not* prepared for what is about to happen.

Well, chaps, what japes shall we get up to today, eh? Who feels like taking the day off to go fishing?!

Whatever is the matter, men?

Th- the thing is, Winker, we have got exams soon. A few of us just thought, maybe, we should go to a few lessons here and there...

BA-HA HA!

You're not joking, are you, chaps? Lessons?! Really?

Et tu, Trotty?

Very well, chaps. That's perfectly alright, don't worry about me. You have, er -- fun, and I'll see you anon.

Anyone seen Winker?

He must know it's dinnertime.

He sent me a wire. Said he'll be dining at his club tonight.

Really?

What have we done?

He's disgusted with us.

Next morning.

There's a special treat this morning, boys! We're going to take the school bus to the girls' school and join them for country dancing.

Dancing?!

W-with girls??

Oh yes!

PROFESSOR POPALOP!

by your old pal **LORENZO!**

BY THE RINGS OF SATURN! PROFESSOR POPALOP'S DECIDED TO SEE IF HIS ASSISTANT, FANGLES, CAN BREATHE IN SPACE, AND SO HAS BUILT HIM A SPECIAL *"ROCKET SHIP"* TO CARRY OUT THE TASK! THE PROFESSOR HAS USED A NUMBER OF *DIFFERENT* ENGINES, BUT ISN'T SURE IF HE HAS ENOUGH *THRUST* YET. THE SHIP NEEDS TO TRAVEL AT 3000MPH. LOOKING AT THE SHIP, AND THE CHART ON THE RIGHT, CAN YOU TELL IF THE PROF HAS ENOUGH *POWER?* AND IF NOT, WHAT ENGINES SHOULD HE ADD TO GET *EXACTLY* 3000MPH?

JUST WHERE DOES THE PROFESSOR GET THE MONEY TO BUY ALL THIS STUFF?

CHALLENGE NUMBER ONE!

BIG BLUE BLASTA

+ 300 MPH PER ENGINE

QUICK DRY GO-GO-GUN

+ 30 MPH PER ENGINE

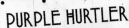

PURPLE HURTLER

+ 200 MPH PER ENGINE

RAGING ROCKETS

+ 210 MPH PER RED ROCKET

+ 130 MPH PER GREEN ROCKET

CHALLENGE NUMBER TWO!

READY FOR TAKE-OFF? GOOD! THE PROF HAS TO ENTER A *SECRET LAUNCH CODE* BEFORE SENDING FANGLES INTO *ORBIT.* USING HIS NOTES ON THE RIGHT CAN YOU FIGURE OUT THE *ORDER* IN WHICH THE BUTTONS MUST BE PRESSED?

CHALLENGE NUMBER THREE!

- ALL NINE BUTTONS MUST EACH BE PRESSED ONCE.
- The seventh button to be pressed is button G.
- Button F can only be pressed directly after button B
- The forth button to be pressed is button I.
- Button D must be pressed between button G and button H.
- Button A can only be pressed directly before button I.
- Button C must be pressed after button E (E is the fifth button).
- Button B is the first button to be pressed.

THE PROF HAS LOST THE KEY TO THE IGNITION! WHICH OF THE KEYS BELOW *EXACTLY* MATCHES THE ONE ABOVE?

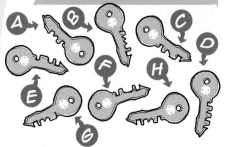

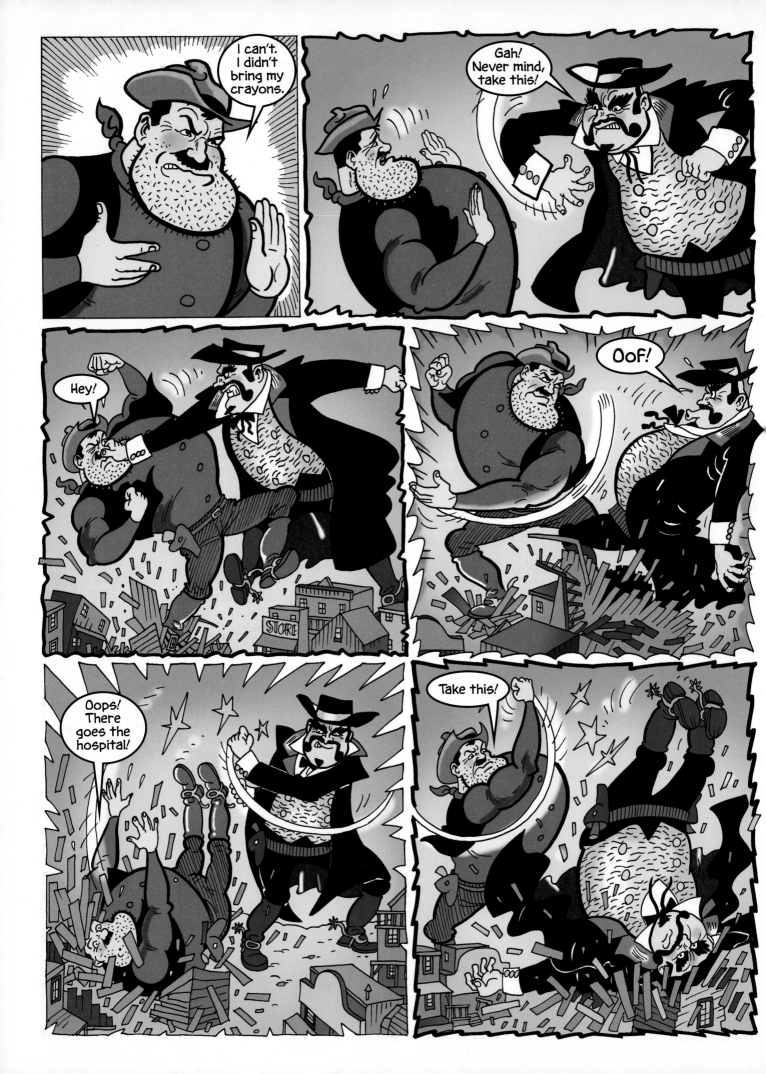